INVESTIGATING
Streams and Rivers

*An Interdisciplinary Curriculum Guide
for Use with Mitchell and Stapp's Field
Manual for Water Quality Monitoring*

*Includes Suggestions for Using
Computer Networks to Enhance Student
Understanding*

Edited by

**William B. Stapp ● Mare M. Cromwell ●
David C. Schmidt ● Andy W. Alm**

Research Contributors

Ruth Fanagan	Yve Susskind
Mark Mitchell	Arjen Wals
Julie Newman	Gregory Zogg

G

K E N [I Y

4050   02

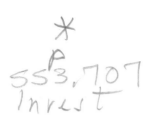

All photos by William B. Stapp unless otherwise credited.

This manual is used in many national and international watershed programs linked through the Global Rivers Environmental Education Network (GREEN). For further information regarding this international network contact:

GREEN
721 E. Huron Street
Ann Arbor, Michigan 48104, USA
Telephone: 313-761-8142
FAX: 313-761-4951
Internet: <green@green.org>
World Wide Web: <http://www.igc.apc.org/green>

People or programs interested in becoming a member of the Global Rivers Environmental Education Network (GREEN) and/or obtaining additional water quality educational materials are encouraged to contact the GREEN Office.

Printed in the United States of America
10 9 8 7 6 5 4 3 2 1

Contents

Introduction
How to Use These Activities   **1**
Approaches for Sharing Ideas and Information Across Your
     Watershed   **4**

PART I: Getting to Know the River
Overview   **13**
Activity 1: Mapping a Watershed   **15**
Activity 2: Stream/River Walk   **23**
Activity 3: Rivers and People   **33**

PART II: Monitoring Water Quality
Overview   **39**
Activity 4: Physical-chemical and Biological Monitoring   **43**
Activity 5: Interpreting the Results   **49**

PART III: Problem-Solving
Overview   **53**
Activity 6: Identifying Specific Problems   **55**
Activity 7: Visualizing the Future   **59**
Activity 8: Selecting an Issue to Address   **63**
Activity 9: Contacting Organizations and Decision Makers   **67**
Activity 10: Developing an Action Plan   **73**
Activity 11: Taking Action   **79**
Activity 12: Follow-Up   **83**
References   **87**

Information About GREEN   **91**

INTRODUCTION
How to Use These Activities

The purpose of these activities is to encourage student inquiry, investigation, and action regarding local streams and rivers. The activities are designed primarily for use in a classroom setting, for students 12-18 years old. However, they could be easily adapted to non-traditional educational settings and, with only slight modifications, most activities would be appropriate for younger or older learners as well. The activities are sequential and organized into three topic areas:

➤ The first section, *Getting to Know the River,* consists of activities which help to orient students to their local watercourse. In **ACTIVITY 1: Mapping a Watershed,** students are introduced to the concept of a watershed and discuss how humans use the river. Students explore their nearby river in **ACTIVITY 2: Stream/River Walk.** They learn about the history of the river by interviewing local people in **ACTIVITY 3: Rivers and People.**

➤ The *Monitoring Water Quality,* section describes how to evaluate a variety of water quality parameters through field testing. It consists of **ACTIVITY 4: Physical-chemical and Biological Monitoring,** and **ACTIVITY 5: Interpreting the Results.**

➤ The *Problem-Solving* section allows students to act on the information they have gathered in previous activities. It begins with **ACTIVITY 6: Identifying Specific Problems** in which students discuss the major problems affecting the river. Students develop visions and goals for the future state of the river in **ACTIVITY 7: Visualizing the Future.** Next, students go through a series of problem-solving steps, including: **ACTIVITY 8: Selecting an Issue to Address, ACTIVITY 9: Contacting Organizations and**

Decision Makers, **ACTIVITY 10: Developing an Action Plan,** and **ACTIVITY 11: Taking Action.** Finally, **ACTIVITY 12: Follow-Up,** offers suggestions for how to help students evaluate and wrap-up their action project.

You will find that the activities follow one another in a logical manner, and there is a carry-over of skills from one activity to the next. The whole program, as described here, will take approximately three to four weeks (3-4 hours of class time per week) to run. However, most of the activities can be used by themselves and in any order that is meaningful and relevant to you. The whole program can certainly take place over a shorter period of time in more concentrated weekly sessions, or over a longer period. Be creative and adapt them freely to suit your needs!

We recommend that you use the activities in conjunction with the **Field Manual for Water Quality Monitoring,** by Mark K. Mitchell and William B. Stapp, published by Kendall/Hunt Publishing Company. This book provides useful information needed to undertake your own water quality monitoring project, including descriptions of the appropriate types of chemical and biological tests you can perform. It also contains important background information on stream ecology, water chemistry, land use practices, international perspectives and computer networking.

However, most of the activities can be used even if you do not have access to a copy of the Field Manual, or if you use a guidebook from another monitoring program. Only **ACTIVITY 4: Physical-chemical and Biological Monitoring** and **ACTIVITY 5: Interpreting the Results** requires the use of the Stapp and Mitchell manual. **ACTIVITY 4** also *requires* the use of specialized water testing equipment. The types of test kits you need and sources to obtain them are listed in Appendix A of the **Field Manual for Water Quality Monitoring.** Copies of the latest edition of this text are available from:

KENDALL/HUNT PUBLISHING COMPANY
4050 Westmark Drive
P.O. Box 1840
Dubuque, Iowa 52004-1840
Tel: 800-228-0810
FAX: 800-772-9165

Special care has been taken to make the activities as easy to use as possible. For each one we highlight important points you will need to know in order to implement them in the classroom, including:

➤   *Objectives*—outlines the learning objectives for the activity.

➤   *Materials*—list of items you need.

➤   *Time*—a recommendation of how long the activity takes.

➤   *Background Information*—describes relevant background information which you may find helpful and provides a rationale for the activity.

➤   *Procedure*—step-by-step guidelines for leading the class.

➤   *Computer Conference Ideas*—suggestions for using computer networks to enhance student understanding.

Approaches for Sharing Ideas and Information Across Your Watershed

The Watershed-wide Approach to Investigating Streams and Rivers

Investigating Streams and Rivers provides a comprehensive collection of activities to help your class study their local environment. Your students can become oriented to their local watershed; gather data on water quality, land use, and the history of the people in their watershed; and develop action plans to address problems they have discovered during their investigation. This program can become even more powerful when you collaborate with teachers and students in other classrooms across your watershed who are also studying the same river system. One of the goals behind *Investigating Streams and Rivers* is for learners to understand their entire watershed system in order to develop appropriate strategies for problem solving and action taking. To achieve this goal, it is helpful to have many groups across your watershed gathering and sharing information and ideas.

The Rouge River Education Program provides a good example of a watershed-wide approach to the study of a single river system. The Rouge River watershed covers 465 square miles in the Detroit metropolitan area. Because of the size of this watershed, it would be very difficult for an individual class to study the land, the river and the people of this entire ecosystem. Therefore, numerous schools have worked together to study this large river system. Currently, there are over 100 schools in this watershed that are investigating the Rouge River system and sharing the information they have gathered with students in other classes. The large collection of watershed data that all of the schools have gathered helps all of the students in the Rouge River Education Program develop a better understanding of their river system.

The Rouge River Education Program has developed and grown for over 10 years. When you begin to use *Investigating Streams and Rivers*, it is not necessary for you to collaborate with so many schools. You can begin by sharing information with one other group within your watershed. In time, who knows how many classrooms may become involved!

Benefits of Sharing Information and Ideas Across your Watershed

There are a number of important benefits your students will appreciate when they are collaborating and sharing information with students in other schools across your watershed.

1. *Understanding the Watershed*
   Watersheds are complex systems that can sometimes cover large geographic areas. To develop a better picture of your system, it is important that information is gathered from all parts of the watershed; from the headwaters down to the mouth. Many river systems begin in rural areas and end in urban centers. Different types of pollution, such as agricultural runoff and industrial waste, can come from these different areas. By gathering and sharing information with other students in the watershed, your students will begin to see how different types of land use affect their river system.

2. *Building a Community of Learners*
   By sharing information and communicating with other students in their watershed, your students will begin to feel that they are a part of a community of learners that goes beyond the walls of their own classroom. They may discover that students outside of their school have similar interests and experiences. By actively participating in this community of learners, your students will develop communication skills that will be essential to their work throughout their lives.

3. *Cross-cultural Sharing and Understanding*
   Because many rivers flow through rural, suburban and urban areas, your students will have the opportunity to communicate with people from a variety of backgrounds, lifestyles and experiences from across their watershed. The students will begin by sharing information and ideas about their common river, however, there will be many opportunities for your students to share information about themselves and their own experiences. Your students will learn about the commonalties and the differences between people throughout their watershed.

Figure 1. Students using school computer to share river data with within the same river basin.

How to Share Ideas and Information Across your Watershed

Communication is an important component of watershed-wide education programs. Students share their water quality data, help each other with data analysis, and share ideas for problem solving and action taking. For watershed education programs that have involved only a few schools that are in the same neighborhood, it has been easy for these teachers and students to gather together to share ideas and information. For programs that involve many schools, or have great distances between schools, the use of computer networks has proven to be a very valuable communication tool.

A computer network is a system that coordinates communication between computer users. Typically a network provides services such as: *electronic mail* or messages to specific individuals or groups; *newsgroups* that allow you to post general e-mail messages on specific topics for your group to read and discuss; and the *World Wide Web,* an Internet-wide program providing links to other text, graphical and interactive resources. In addition, a new database program, *RiverBank,* has been developed that allows users to enter and evaluate their watershed data, then exchange data files on-line.

Computer networks can provide tremendous opportunities for communication among student groups involved in investigating streams and rivers. In particular, participating in a newsgroup or computer conference can enhance student understanding of concepts learned through the activities in this curriculum guide and can foster local, regional and international communication.

Choosing the Best Tools for On-line Communication

When sharing ideas and information on-line, it is important to choose the appropriate means of communication for your particular situation. For example, how should you share water quality data with others in your watershed? Listed below are several methods for on-line communication and some suggestions for how they can be used.

RiverBank Database

A new computer software tool created by The University of Michigan and the Global Rivers Environmental Education Network (GREEN) will help teachers and students share and analyze the water quality and land-use data they have gathered. RiverBank fills the need for a long term data storage and data sharing tool that is easy to use. It has a user friendly interface allowing easy input of monitoring site surveys, benthic survey results, and results from the nine chemical-physical water quality tests. RiverBank provides a standardized format for transmission and storage of watershed monitoring data via electronic mail or the World Wide Web.

Conferences and Newsgroups

On-line group news and discussion forums help students, teachers and professionals in countries all over the world interact by sharing observations about the watershed, discussing technical and policy questions, sending personal messages, and disseminating the results of interviews, student poetry, and other creative writing. The use of on-line group forums in a watershed education program can help to create a "community" of people interested and concerned about their river. These forums also provide a permanent, written record of interaction among participants in a watershed project that can be printed and shared with others.

GREEN has created a collection of computer forums that are accessible on the Internet in several ways: as mailing lists to which anyone may subscribe, and as newsgroups accessible to subscribers on specific networks such as EcoNet in the United States and Pegasus Networks in Australia. Students and teachers in countries all over the world are able to interact and share ideas, thoughts and feelings related to water quality issues via these forums. Special-purpose conferences have been (and can be) organized through GREEN to facilitate in-depth communication among members of a given watershed or special project.

Figure 2. Three Russian students communicating with their Cross Cultural Watershed Partner School in Dayton, Ohio, USA. (Photo by Heike Mainhardt)

GREEN's on-line forums are continually changing to keep up with educators' needs and changes in technology. For further information on GREEN sponsored on-line forums, hardware and software options, and choices for Internet service providers, contact:

Global Rivers Environmental Education Network
721 E. Huron
Ann Arbor, Michigan 48104 USA

phone: 313-761-8142
fax: 313-761-4951
e-mail: green@green.org

World Wide Web

The World Wide Web (WWW) is an exciting and visually pleasing way to explore the many resources available on the Internet. WWW pages are places on the Internet where you can find information, on-line interaction and links to other locations on the Internet. GREEN's site on the WWW is used to share information with participants throughout the GREEN network and is a great place for students to begin to search for and share information on river studies and related topics. School and community groups that create their own WWW sites to publish information about their watershed education programs can have their pages linked to GREEN's WWW site at: <http://www.igc.apc.org/green>.

Keys to Successful On-line Learning

Using computer networks takes practice. There are few shortcuts, and even most of the main roads are "under construction." Computer networks are relatively new and are experiencing phenomenal growth; there are still a lot of rough edges, and things frequently break under the strain.

So the fundamental lesson in computer networking for your watershed education program is patience. Painting false expectations of the tremendous resources available on the networks can lead to discouragement among participants, and outright hostility toward the technology, if the way to those resources is too rough. Once frustrated, a would-be networker is less likely to try again.

Some key elements identified for success in building electronic communities are good to keep in mind when considering on-line communication (Riel and Levin, 1990). They are summarized and explained below.

> ➤ Use of computer networks must be relatively easy. Users need access to the technical equipment, software, training, and support for sending and receiving messages. They also need the time and social support for such activity. If using a computer network is an added burden in an educator's already overloaded schedule, it won't happen.

> ➤ There must be strong incentives for using computer networks. This type of communication must be more efficient or productive than other kinds of research or interaction.

> ➤ For a group to function well in an on-line environment, it needs to share specific goals or tasks. There must be clear expectations of the requirements for responding to messages.

> ➤ Someone must take responsibility for facilitating on-line interaction.

Ease of Use

How "easy" on-line networking is for the individual user depends on several factors. First, the computer used for networking must be accessible. If telecommunication requires a trip down the hall, or staying up late at night to take advantage of low-cost phone rates, it is less likely that telecommunications will be integrated into the regular routine of an educator or student. So convenience is a key consideration in planning for success in telecomputing.

Second, the simpler the computer hardware, software, and telecommunications service is to use, the likelier it is to be employed. Low-cost equipment, software, and services may look like a bargain, but they can be discouraging.

Incentives

Unless there is a strong perceived need or value in computer networking, people will choose other ways to communicate and to find information. Likewise, disincentives like cost and the time required to use a new technology can block success, if the value of using the technology is unclear. Sometimes, an incentive may be simple: Access to timely information that may not arrive for days or weeks by mail, or the ability to correspond quickly to meet an important deadline, can be great motivators for using computer networks.

Setting Goals, Tasks, and Rules

Without clear strategies for using on-line communication the technology can easily become a hindrance rather than a help. To make effective use of the technology, whether in a classroom, training session, or in an interactive on-line project, setting goals, measurable objectives, timelines, and rules or expectations are essential.

Goals for on-line communication may be broadly stated, but they should reflect the needs of and purposes for the effort. "We will use computer networks to access information resources that are not available locally," or "This project will use a computer conference to share environmental monitoring data among participants at geographically dispersed sites," are examples of goal statements.

Objectives are more specific. They generally provide the "who, what, and when" for tasks. "By the end of the training, participants will have used the World Wide Web to access a variety of information resources on water pollution," or "Each participant in this project is expected to respond to electronic mail from other project participants within 48 hours," are examples. An objective should be stated so that evaluation of success is straightforward—either it was met or it wasn't. By sharing or even co-developing objectives with a group prior to an activity, all participants can form a common understanding of purpose. This is especially important when they are communicating only via computer networks, without the same group dynamic that develops in face-to-face situations.

Suggestions for Sharing Ideas and Information

At the end of each activity in this manual are suggestions for using computer networks as an extension of that activity. Included are specific examples of the types of ideas and information you will be sharing on *GREEN* sponsored forums and GREEN's WWW site. Our experience has shown that people are more likely to actively participate in a computer network if they feel they have something to share. The activities in this curriculum guide all end with some "product" or set of observations that could serve as topics of communication between student groups.

To help you plan and organize classroom activities, the following table lists the 12 activities included in this curriculum, and the associated 15 topics (i.e., items of discussion) for you to share with other teachers and students in your watershed on a GREEN on-line forum or via e-mail. To improve your likelihood of success in using on-line forums, make sure you have clearly established mutual objectives and timelines for activities with partners and teachers or youth leaders. Also be sure to decide ahead of time who is responsibility for facilitating or leading each on-line activity.

Table of Curriculum Activities and Associated Discussion Topics

CURRICULUM ACTIVITIES		DISCUSSION TOPICS	
Mapping a Watershed	ACTIVITY 1	TOPIC 1	Introduction to the River Study
		TOPIC 2	Members of the River Study
		TOPIC 3	The Watershed Concept
Stream/River Walk	ACTIVITY 2	TOPIC 4	Describe your Section of the Watershed
		TOPIC 5	The Field Data Sheet
Rivers and People	ACTIVITY 3	TOPIC 6	River History
Physical-chemical and Biological Monitoring	ACTIVITY 4	TOPIC 7	Water Quality Monitoring Data
Interpreting the Results	ACTIVITY 5	TOPIC 8	Analyzing the Data
Identifying Specific Problems	ACTIVITY 6	TOPIC 9	Specific Problems in the Watershed
Visualizing the Future	ACTIVITY 7	TOPIC 10	Future Visions for the Watershed
Selecting an Issue to Address	ACTIVITY 8	TOPIC 11	Selecting an Issue for Further Investigation
Contacting Organizations and Decision Makers	ACTIVITY 9	TOPIC 12	Resources for Gathering and Information
Developing an Action Plan	ACTIVITY 10	TOPIC 13	Actions to Improve Water Quality
Taking Action	ACTIVITY 11	TOPIC 14	Taking Action: Opportunities and Constraints
Follow-Up	ACTIVITY 12	TOPIC 15	Evaluation

PART I

Getting to Know the River

Overview

Viewed from space, the earth is often called the "blue planet" because almost two-thirds of its surface is covered by water. This great abundance of water is unique in the solar system; without it, there would be no life on our planet. Most of this water is contained in the oceans and the polar ice caps. However, water can also be found in lakes and glaciers; stored in the ground as groundwater and soil moisture; in the atmosphere as clouds or rain; in plants and animals; and in streams and rivers. The total amount of water on the earth is constant. It may change form, or be transported from one place to another, but water is never lost or gained on a planetary scale. This movement of water—for example, from clouds to a river, or from a river to the ocean—is called the **hydrologic cycle.**

All forms of life rely either directly or indirectly upon water for their survival. This is especially true of humans, who require good, clean water not just for drinking, but for almost every other aspect of their lives, including: agriculture, bathing, washing clothes, sewers and sanitation, industry, etc. Streams and rivers are often the primary source of much of the water that we use. Typically, they are the most tangible evidence of freshwater around us.

Despite the apparent abundance of water on the globe—remember that most of the earth's surface is covered in water—there are some places where the supply is limited. More importantly, in many countries where water supplies are adequate the quality of the water is poor. Pollution can make pure water undrinkable and even dangerous to touch.

Where does the water that you use come from? How do you and the people that live in your community use nearby rivers or streams? What is the water quality like in the area where you live? Was it always that way?

These are some of the questions we will ask ourselves as we explore our river through the following activities:

➤ *Activity 1:* Mapping a Watershed

➤ *Activity 2:* Stream/River Walk

➤ *Activity 3:* Rivers and People

Activity

Mapping a Watershed

Objectives

- Understand the concept of a watershed (catchment)
- Map the boundaries of a local watershed
- Show the locations of the channels that form your river system
- Locate significant natural features within the water-shed
- Ilustrate major land uses within the watershed

Materials

- United States Geographical Survey maps, road maps, topographical maps, satellite maps, or land use maps (if available)

- pencils
- crayons or colored pencils
- paper (preferably for tracing)

Time

 approximately 80 minutes

Background Information

As a first step in getting to know and understand a river or a stream, we must figure out where the water comes from. If precipitation exceeds evaporation in a given area, water will collect, and either move into the ground, or travel along its surface. Water draining from many such land surfaces form channels, called **streams.** Streams may also form from underground springs, marshes, melting glaciers, lake outlets, or summer monsoons. Streams join together to form large watercourses called **rivers,** much like branches join together to form a trunk of a tree.

Every river is part of a **river system,** or network, which includes all the other streams and rivers which flow into it. Rivers are also closely tied to the land which is around them. Remember that water draining from the surface of the ground, or below it, flows into streams and rivers. The land area that drains the water into a river system is called a **watershed or catchment.** It is the drainage basin of a river system and includes the entire landscape which surrounds a river, as well as the channels which make up the river.

Every person on earth lives within a watershed. Someone once said that "a river is a memory of the land through which it flows." To understand a local river or stream, we must understand its watershed.

Procedure

1. Locate a local stream or river on a map.

   a. In the U.S.A., United States Geographical Survey (USGS) Maps are often easiest to use for this activity; they show greater detail than a road map.

   b. Satellite maps may not be as detailed as a USGS Map, but may be used to locate your stream or river and land use patterns (note Figures 3 and 4).

   c. Make sure your map includes the entire watershed.

2. Select a spot on the map, as far downstream as possible, for your starting point. Next, locate the upstream ends of all channels that flow into your river above that point.

3. Draw a line that includes all of the branches or tributaries of your stream or river. This is your watershed. Be sure to separate it from other watersheds (see example below).

4. Locate or draw on the map significant natural features (including forests, grasslands, deserts, mountains, valleys, plateaus, ridges, lakes, marshes, deltas, farmland, communities, roads, impoundments, etc.).

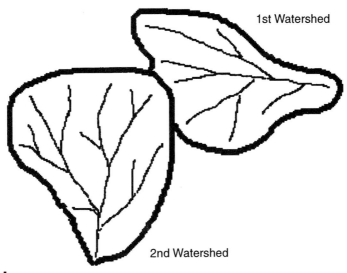

1st Watershed

2nd Watershed

| Example of Watershed Diagram

5. Identify on the map the major land uses within the watershed (such as industry, agriculture, residential neighborhoods, or commercial development). General Development Maps and Zoning Maps, available from county and township governments in the U.S. are helpful in identifying land use. Or simply draw on your and the students' knowledge of your region to identify land uses.

6. Consider the following questions for discussion:

    a. Where does the water in your watershed come from (rain and snow, groundwater, glacial meltwater, from wetlands, etc.)? Are the streams and rivers in the watershed present all year round, or do they dry up during hot seasons?

    b. What are some of the major land uses in your watershed (consult your map)? How might these different land uses effect the river?

    c. How would human activities in one part of the watershed, for example dumping of sewage or industrial wastes, effect other parts of the watershed?

Figure 3. Satellite map of the Rouge River flowing into the Detroit River.

Figure 4. Satellite map of the Lower and Main Branch of the Rouge River discharging to the Detroit River.

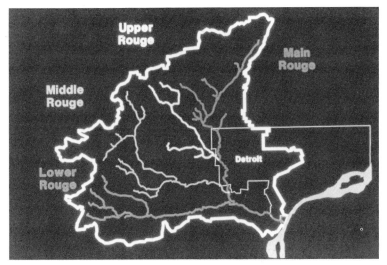

| Figure 5. Map of the Rouge River Watershed containing the four major branches.

Sharing Information
Computer Network Ideas

When you first begin to share ideas and information with other schools in your watershed, you should start by introducing the river study program and outlining some of the goals and objectives for your on-line communication. Topic 1 is an example of a message you may send as e-mail, or post to a computer conference or newsgroup.

Topic 1

Introduction to the River Study

Welcome to our watershed conference! This computer conference has been designed by GREEN (the Global Rivers Environmental Education Network) to foster communication between school groups and individuals within our watershed.

The goals for our on-line communication are for you to:

◆ share your thoughts and feelings about water quality issues in your community and throughout the entire watershed.

Topic 1—continued

◆ compare the water quality monitoring data that you will collect from your local stream or river with that collected by other school groups or individuals.

◆ discuss your visions for the future state of rivers within the watershed, and the types of actions you can take to make those visions a reality.

The following series of 15 topics have been developed by GREEN:

TOPIC 1	Introduction to the River Study
TOPIC 2	Members of the River Study
TOPIC 3	The Watershed Concept
TOPIC 4	Describe Your Section of the Watershed
TOPIC 5	The Field Data Sheet
TOPIC 6	River History
TOPIC 7	Water Quality Monitoring Data
TOPIC 8	Analyzing the Data
TOPIC 9	Specific Problems in the Watershed
TOPIC 10	Future Visions for the Watershed
TOPIC 11	Selecting an Issue for Further Investigation
TOPIC 12	Resources for Gathering Information
TOPIC 13	Actions to Improve Water Quality
TOPIC 14	Taking Actions: Opportunities and Constraints
TOPIC 15	Evaluation

We recommend that you explore and respond to each of the fifteen topics at least one time according to the schedule you received in the mail. We also ask you to create at least one topic to discuss additional issues which are of interest to you during the next three weeks.

Just as land use and natural features vary throughout a watershed, so do the types of human communities found there. As a means of introducing themselves to others in your watershed, your students could describe their school and community (Topic 2). Why are they involved in a water quality monitoring project?

Topic 2
Members of the Watershed Education Project

Use this topic to introduce yourself to the rest of the members of the watershed education project. Make sure you include the following information in your introduction:

Name of your school or organization.
Your name.
Number of people in your group and their ages (or grade level).
Name of the river or stream you will be monitoring.
A brief description of the community you live in.
Why you are involved in a water quality monitoring program.
What you hope to learn from being involved in this program.

The concept of a watershed is often difficult to understand. It is a complex idea, but a very important one. Sharing ideas with other school groups may serve as a first step in helping your class gain a better understanding of the interconnectedness of people and water quality issues within a watershed.

Under Topic 3 in the computer conference, your class can contact other students to discuss the watershed concept: Why is it important? What does it mean to them?

Topic 3
The Watershed Concept

◆ Why is the concept of a watershed important?
◆ What are the major land uses within the Saginaw watershed which might have an effect on water quality?
◆ What potential effects could they have?

Because Topic 3 is the first true discussion topic in the conference or newsgroup your students may be somewhat apprehensive. When they compose responses they can imagine they are writing to or talking with a friend. Use the questions provided with each topic as guidelines, but include or omit information as you deem appropriate.

Activity

Stream/River Walk

Objectives

- Engage students in a visual survey of a river or stream that involves mapping and recording information
- Stimulate students to see the river or stream in new ways
- Uncover potential sources of pollution that should be further studied
- Learn methods of how to communicate locations and points on maps to others

Materials

- Clipboards
- pencils
- copies of the "Field Data Sheet" (one is included with this activity)
- map developed in Activity 1

- transportation to the river/stream
- (Optional: zoning, land ownership, and historical maps and aerial photographs of the watershed)

Time

approximately 120 minutes total; 40 minutes each to complete the narrative, stream walk and classroom activities

---

Background Information

In ACTIVITY 1 your entire watershed was the focus of interest. In this activity you have the opportunity to explore a much smaller portion of the watershed, a segment of a local stream or river called a **reach**.

On your stream or river walk you will investigate specific details about the water quality and local land uses of your reach, including: color and appearance of the water; signs of fish and other organisms; potential pollution sources, such as discharge pipes, dumps, or construction sites; and the nature of the stream or river bottom.

It may be difficult in some areas to get to the river bank, or to walk along the river. Or the river may be too wide or deep to see the river bottom, or the opposite side. However, we encourage you to explore and investigate as best you can. You may be surprised at what you find!

This activity has three components: a *narrative* account by the students of their walk; a *stream walk map*; and *classroom activities*.

Procedure

1. Narrative—The narrative is a written account of the stream or river walk. Richness of detail about land uses bordering the watercourse, about colors and odors, about human usage of the river, about suspected pollution sources, and about their perceptions of being at the river emerges from narratives. The narrative is most effective when students use descriptive language that gives color and texture to their perceptions.

    a. Designate stream or river reaches for student groups to walk and survey. Visit potential sites before exploring with the students. Use the following criteria when selecting reaches:

        1) Accessibility and safety are two important criteria to consider when selecting reaches. Be certain to obtain permission if the river access is on or through private land.

        2) Each reach should be bounded by conspicuous reference points such as bridges, monuments, or distinctive natural features, so that students know where the reaches they will investigate begin and end. (Consulting a detailed local map is helpful at this stage.)

        3) Half a kilometer (.3 miles) is a good length for each reach, but you should modify lengths based upon the conditions at your site.

4) Stream or river reaches should be coded or labeled. This will help you to organize the results from each student group. The labeled segment could include the first two letters of the river or stream name, e.g. "RO" for Rouge River. This would be followed by a number that indicates relative position along the stream or river. The segment at the mouth of the Rouge River, USA might be labeled "RO1," the next segment upriver would be labeled "RO2," and so on.

b. Have students explore their reach, noting their thoughts, feelings and impressions in journals or notebooks on-site.

c. Encourage creativity and emphasize feelings and perceptions about the river. You will have ample opportunity to be more analytical in other parts of this activity.

2. **Stream Walk Map**—Students will generate simple maps of their reaches. Each student group can be given its own hand-drawn, photocopied or mimeographed copy of a detailed base map, showing prominent landmarks. Make sure the scale of the map is such that each reach is shown in sufficient detail (if necessary, enlarge the map). Students can create symbols of their own to denote land uses and human-made structures, as long as the whole class utilizes the same system.

a. As each student group walks along a reach, bordering land uses should be noted on their maps: urban areas, industry, residential neighborhoods, agricultural uses, woodlands, etc.

1) Also note features such as islands, bridges, dams, and other barriers in the watercourse.

2) Record inputs to stream flow, such as discharge pipes, open sewers, ditches and other streams, rivers and channels.

3) Finally, direction of flow should be marked on the map, as well as which direction is north.

b. Have each group fill out the "Field Data Sheet" as they walk. (A copy is at end of this Activity). Consult the "Guide to the Field Data Sheet" (also provided with this activity) for information on how to interpret results from the student's field work.

3. **Classroom Activities**

a. Once all groups have collected their data, have them add their findings to a large scale watershed map. Use colored pencils

Figure 6. Examining the channelized section of the Rouge River for sources of pollution and life forms in the River.

or crayons to illustrate major land uses and other results from the field work.

b. Have each group report to the entire class what they found in their reach, including information recorded on the Field Data Sheet.

c. Share passages from student narratives.

d. Discuss the meaning of all these results:

1) What do students think about the river? How do they feel about its current state?

2) Based upon their field work, or things they learned elsewhere, what are some potential problems facing the river today?

3) Did they discover any potential sources of pollution?

4) Is there any evidence of human activities which alter the flow or course of the river (channelization, dams, etc.)?

Figure 7. Students developed a map of the river with photographs, drawings, and articles for a traveling exhibit.

Sharing Information
Computer Network Ideas

Computer networking can be a very powerful tool for helping students to understand water quality issues throughout the entire watershed. Topic 4 on the conference asks students to describe their section of the watershed. It is a valuable opportunity for students to analyze and summarize their stream/river walk. What signs of human impact on the river were visible at their site; e.g., sewage outflow pipes, dumping of trash, etc.?

Have your students review responses from other school groups. Consider the following questions: How do the sites and their nearby land uses differ between upstream and downstream sections of the river? What social, economical and political factors might contribute to these differences?

Topic 4

Describe your Section of the Watershed

Every member of the conference is monitoring water quality at one specific location within the watershed. Please describe your section of the watershed by answering the following questions:

1. What is the name of your School or Organization?
2. Describe where your section is located within the watershed. (What is the name of your stream or river? What are the nearest towns, villages or cities? Be creative and describe your location as best as you can.)
3. Where does the water in your section of the watershed come from (rainwater, groundwater, wetlands, glacial meltwater, etc.)?
4. Describe your site.
5. What are the major land uses in your section?
6. What are the major sources of pollution? (If you don't know what they are as a result of actually visiting your river, try to imagine what the major sources of pollution might be, due to the types of land use in your area.)

Students could also discuss what they learned from using the "Field Data Sheet" with individuals at other schools. Have students enter their results from the "Field Data Sheet" directly into the *RiverBank* Stream Survey Page (see the example below). Compare data from a wide variety of sites in the watershed.

─── *Topic 5* ───

The Field Data Sheet

This topic is for people to share even more information about their section of the watershed, after they have visited a local stream or river. Describe for other members of the conference what your stream or river is like. How large is it? What color is the water? Does it have any odor? Are there any plants or animals in or near the water? For what purposes do humans use the river here? What do you think about the quality of the water at your site?

Use *RiverBank* to record and send the data recorded on your Field Data Sheet.

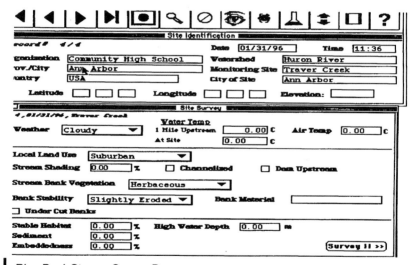

RiverBank Stream Survey Page

Field Data Sheet

Country _____

State, Region, or Province _____

City, Town or Village _____

Watershed _____ Stream or River_____

Reach _____ Date _____

Investigators _____

Today's Weather _____

Yesterday's Weather _____

Use this sheet as a checklist to identify what colors, smells, etc. are found in your reach. For each item you check off, write down any important information about it that you can at the bottom of the page—for example, "the foam in our reach was almost a foot high, and was found right below a big pipe." Record any other significant features you observe or notice.

Water Appearance
_____ green
_____ orange-red
_____ foam
_____ muddy/cloudy
_____ milky/white
_____ multi-colored (oily sheen)
_____ reds, purples, blues, blacks
_____ other

Odors
_____ rotten egg (sulfur)
_____ musky
_____ harsh/bitter/acrid
_____ chlorine
_____ other

Stream/River bottom
_____ rocky
_____ silt/soft
_____ gravel
_____ other

Habitats (the places where plants and animals could live)
_____ pool
_____ riffle/rapids
_____ wetlands
_____ rocks
_____ log piles
_____ weed beds
_____ undercut banks
_____ human-made objects (pilings, bridges)
_____ other

Human Usages
_____ drinking
_____ bathing
_____ washing clothes
_____ waste disposal
_____ transportation (ferries, barges)
_____ watering livestock
_____ recreation (fishing, swimming, boating)
_____ other

General Comments:

_____

_____

_____

_____

Guide to the "Field Data Sheet"

Indicators—Water Appearance

Green: may indicate an overabundance of algae caused by enrichment of the stream. Fertilizer runoff from fields, inadequate sewage treatment, and animal wastes are common sources

Orange/Red: may indicate acid mine drainage, oil well runoff, natural staining due to source headwaters in swamps rich in tannin or iron, or blood from processing plants

Foam: if white and higher than 7-8 cm. above water surface, foam is generally caused by detergents. Thinner surface foam may be a mixture of natural oils and soil particles or pollen

Muddy/Cloudy: may indicate erosion and sedimentation in those streams and rivers that are not naturally muddy. Construction sites, dredging activities, activity of bottom feeders like carp, farmland erosion, logging, and road-building are common contributors

Milky/White: may indicate glacial sources of water, pulp and paper mill discharges, or dairy operations

Multi-Color: may indicate oil floating on the surface from human dumping or oil well operations

Dark reds, purples, blues, and blacks: may indicate dyes from leather tanning, printing operations, clothing manufacturing, etc.

Indicators—Odors

rotten egg (sulfur): indicates sewage pollution

musky: indicates the presence of untreated sewage, livestock waste, or excess algal growth and decay

harsh/bitter/acrid: indicates industrial wastes

chlorine: the smell of chlorine may indicate excessive chlorination of waste effluent

Activity

Rivers and People

Objectives

- Develop interviewing skills
- Design a questionnaire
- Compile the results of interviews and piece together the history of the river

Materials

- pencil
- paper
- tape recorder (optional)

Time

approximately 80 minutes; 40 minutes to design questionnaire and 40 minutes to discuss results (students should do the actual interviews outside of class)

Background Information

Rivers and streams are the focal points of human activity around the world: people fish in the Danube delta; sail feluccas on the Nile River; bathe in the Ganga to wash away sins; take precious water from the Murray River in Australia for irrigation; and guide barges up the Mississippi River. These images reinforce our awareness of the strong connection that exists between people and rivers. People who live close to the natural world come to know local watercourses intimately. Within every watershed and along every

Figure 8. Egyptians use water from irrigation canals for domestic chores and growing crops.

river, there are people who have watched rivers flow for most of their lives. These people have inside them a knowledge about the community and river that is just waiting to be tapped.

In this activity, students will interview people so as to learn more about the river. History comes alive through interviews. Discussions with real people about their impressions and experiences with the river is often much more meaningful than simply reading a book or article

Procedure

1. Have students work alone or in groups to develop a series of questions they would like to ask someone about the river or stream. Below are some sample questions:

   How long have you lived in this area?

   What do you remember the river being like when you were my age?

   Did you use the river in different ways than we use it now?

   What are your feelings about the river today?

   What are your hopes for the river in the future?

Figure 9. Water from a local river in Bombay, India is directed to land and used by laundry washers and then returned to the river system.

Figure 10. Interview of Japanese residents along the Minamata River in Kyushu, Japan regarding Minamata Disease from Mercury contamination.

2. Have students interview several people about the river (they can do this as a homework assignment over a weekend, or perhaps over the course of an entire week.) The following suggestions will help students to conduct an effective interview:

   a. Try to interview older people, who may have a lot of knowledge about local history. Family members and neighbors may be a good place to start in recruiting people to interview.

   b. Inform the person you are planning to interview, of the purpose of the interview, how long it will last, and how the interview results will be used.

   c. Give them an idea of the types of questions you will be asking.

   d. Role-play interviewing other students before conducting the real interviews.

   e. Try to draw out specific examples from people who make general statements. For example, if someone were to tell you that they used to play in the river, ask them "What exactly did you do in the river? Did you swim, fish, collect bugs, etc.?"

3. Have students discuss their results. Consider some of the following questions:

   How do the students' views of the river differ from those of the people whom they interviewed?

   In what ways is the river of today like the river of yesterday (10, 20, 30, 40 years ago)? How is it different?

   How do the people who were interviewed feel about the river?

   Were there any commonalties in their experiences with the river? How did their experiences differ?

   Compare and contrast the ways in which people use the river today from how it was used in the past.

4. Consider compiling the interviews into a booklet. If possible find old pictures that can complement the text. The people interviewed may allow the use of personal photographs or old newspaper clippings, or can direct students to such resources. Below are excerpts from interviews about river landings along the Mississippi River conducted by students from Brussels Community High School, Brussels, Illinois, USA. These interviews were part of a collection of student poetry, stories, river recipes, and personal interviews that were compiled in a book called *Meanderings:*

   "From about 1910 to 1930, we took livestock to [the] river to be sold. We either hauled it in a wagon or drove the livestock [by] horseback. A bunch of farmers got together to do this . . ."

   —Eileen Friedel

"Many stores relied on the river for produce and crops for business . . . Once in a while, when the river froze up in the winter, they didn't get much business."

—Albert Baalman

Sharing Information
Computer Network Ideas

Computer networking can lead to a better understanding of the relationship between people and the river or watershed. Students can enter the results of their interviews into the computer conference, thus sharing the personal experiences that local people have had with the river with an even greater audience. After reviewing the responses from other school groups have your students consider the questions: How is the river used differently today than it was in the past? Why? In what parts of the watershed have these changes in human activities been most significant?

Topic 6
River History

Share some information about the history of your local river, following the suggestions given below:

1. Describe what you know about the history of your area, and what role the river may have played in it.

2. If you or members of your group interviewed local people about the river, summarize some of the most interesting things you learned.

3. How has the water quality changed over the last 100 years?

4. Do humans use the river for different purposes today than they did 10, 20, 30, 40, 50 or more years ago? If so, how might these changes in use effect water quality?

PART II

Monitoring Water Quality

Overview

As a result of their investigations (Activities 1, 2, and 3) or prior experiences with local rivers, your students may be full of questions: "How "clean" is the river? Is water that looks "clean" actually "clean"? Is water that looks dirty really polluted? What influence does local land use patterns actually have on water quality? How does water upstream compare with the water downstream in the river?" Answers to these and other questions can be found through involvement in a water testing program and communication with other members of your watershed.

Two major approaches that students could use to monitor and evaluate water quality are:

1) **physical-chemical testing,** which involves measuring vari ous physical and chemical parameters in the river, or
2) **biological monitoring,** which uses living organisms as an indicator of water quality.

Sources of pollution, and other factors which affect water quality, are so diverse that using both methods of monitoring is better than using just one method exclusively. For example, physical-chemical testing, such as measuring dissolved oxygen can reveal the presence of oxygen demanding wastes like raw sewage. But it cannot indicate toxic contamination from sources like heavy metals. For this, we can use biological methods, like counting and identifying large, bottom-dwelling invertebrates (mostly insects), called **benthic macroinvertebrates,** that are sensitive to these wastes.

Coupling the biological monitoring and physical-chemical testing approaches insures that the majority of environmental insults to local streams and rivers are detected. Determining the status of the river is the first step in correcting the problem!

Worksheet for Calculating the Overall Water
Quality of the Section of a River System

Parameters	Weighting Factor Column A	Weighting Curve Value Column B	Total Column C
1. Dissolved Oxygen	0.17	70	11.9
2. Fecal Coliform Density	0.16	65	10.4
3. pH	0.11	80	8.8
4. B.O.D.	0.11	70	7.7
5. Nitrates	0.10	65	6.5
6. Phosphorus	0.10	40	4.0
7. Temperature	0.10	75	7.5
8. Turbidity	0.08	80	6.4
9. Total Dissolved Solids	0.07	65	4.55

Overall Water Quality Index 66.75

Figure 11. Data from a section of the middle portion of the Cuyahoga River in Cleveland, Ohio.

You will need to use the **Field Manual for Water Quality Monitoring,** by Mark K. Mitchell and William B. Stapp (or some other monitoring sourcebook) in order to guide you and your students through the sampling in **Activity 4: Physical-chemical and Biological Monitoring,** and data analysis in **Activity 5: Interpreting the Results.** The Stapp and Mitchell manual (published by Kendall/Hunt) are now used in projects in over 135 countries throughout the world. It is a valuable resource, and provides information needed to undertake your own project.

The water quality monitoring program described in the manual is designed around the National Sanitation Foundation's Water Quality Index. Nine water quality tests are conducted, including:

➤ dissolved oxygen,

➤ fecal coliform (critical measurement for the presence of animal and human wastes)

➤ pH

➤ biochemical oxygen demand (a five day measurement of the oxygen demand of microorganisms in the water)

➤ temperature

➤ total phosphates

➤ nitrates

➤ turbidity

➤ total solids.

Data from the nine tests is used to calculate an overall Water Quality Index—a single number (0-100) representing water quality at the sampling site. The Index is a useful tool for monitoring changes in water quality over time, to compare water quality of different river segments, and to share results with other river systems around the world.

Models for sampling and monitoring benthic macroinvertebrates are also described in detail in the Field Manual for Water Quality Monitoring (Kendall/Hunt Publishing Company).

➤ *Activity 4:* Physical-Chemical and Biological Monitoring

➤ *Activity 5:* Interpreting the Results

Activity

Physical-chemical and Biological Monitoring

Objectives

- Learn the meanings and procedures of nine physical-chemical tests
- Learn one or more methods of biological monitoring
- Follow prescribed safety guidelines for testing and sampling

Materials

- chemical test kits
- benthic collection equipment
- other miscellaneous equipment described in the **Field Manual for Water Quality Monitoring**

Time

approximately 180 minutes total; 80-120 minutes to teach the tests; 80 minutes to sample

---

Background Information

Below we offer some suggestions to help you organize and administer your water quality monitoring project. However, these are meant only as helpful hints at planning. You will need to read and follow directions in the **Field Manual for Water Quality Monitoring,** by Mark K. Mitchell and William B. Stapp. In the book you will find information on the procedures for each test, as well as how to interpret your results. In addition, important safety guidelines are outlined in detail. Review these carefully, as safety must be your primary concern!

Procedure

Physical-chemical Tests

1. Initial preparation

   a. Review the **Field Manual for Water Quality Monitoring.** Familiarize yourself with each test and important safety recommendations.

   b. Inventory test equipment to make sure you have everything you need (Consult the equipment list enclosed with each test kit).

   c. For safety purposes we also recommend you have on hand:

      1) safety goggles for each student

      2) first aid kit

      3) eye wash bottle

      4) plastic gloves

      5) clean pail or bucket for washing hands

      6) water for washing (not from stream or river)

      7) soap (biodegradable if possible)

      8) towels

      9) waste container for empty "powder pillows"

      10) waste container for liquid chemical waste

      11) waste container labeled "hazardous waste" for nitrate "powder pillows", cadmium particles, and liquid nitrate waste)— this must be disposed of in accordance with hazardous waste guidelines; contact science department at your school or local university.

2. Teaching students the tests

   a. Have your students read "Chapter 3: Meaning of the Tests" in the **Field Manual for Water Quality Monitoring.** If the material is too difficult for your students, consider creating information sheets that summarize each test, or simply describe the tests to them.

   b. Have students perform each test at least once, so they will gain some familiarity with testing and safety procedures. If possible, have the students progress to different "stations" where they will learn one or more tests at a time. This will require additional teaching assistance in the classroom.

| **Figure 12.** Use of safety goggles while testing for dissolved oxygen.

c. Although it is important to familiarize each student with all of the tests, it is often helpful to have them become *proficient* at only one test, or at most several tests. This way you can insure greater accuracy in testing in the field. Also, students will become "experts" on specific tests, and can act as resource people for the entire class.

d. Divide students into teams which will be responsible for performing a specific test(s). Make sure each student is aware of his/her responsibilities. Ideally each team would practice its test(s) once as a group indoors before going out in the field.

3. Field Testing

a. Visit the site before the testing date. Determine the easiest access to the site, any potential safety hazards, and where sampling will take place. Be certain to obtain permission from private land owners.

b. If necessary, be sure to obtain assistance from other teachers or chaperons on the test day.

c. Remind students constantly of important safety considerations: use gloves and goggles, safe sampling techniques, and proper waste disposal.

d. Have fun!

Figure 13. Collecting aquatic insects and placing in an enamel pan for identification.

Biological Monitoring

1. Biological monitoring of benthic macroinvertebrates can be more difficult to use and understand than physical-chemical tests. But it can also be exciting and rewarding. Many students will marvel at the variety of life forms evident in a river or stream. First read "Chapter 6: Benthic Macroinvertebrates" in the **Field Manual for Water Quality Monitoring,** in order to gain a better understanding of the procedures involved in biological monitoring. Then, based upon your skills and student interest, decide which methods you might use. The Field Manual (or another resource) will be helpful as a guide to learn the distinguishing characteristics of the common macroinvertebrates prior to visiting the stream.

2. Any equipment you might need is discussed in the manual.

3. Planning and preparation for field sampling of benthics can be coordinated with the preparation for field testing, or done as a separate unit.

Sharing Information
Computer Network Ideas

This topic is used to instruct the River Study participants on the procedures for sharing their water quality data. There are many different ways of organizing this data sharing activity. One example can be found below.

Topic 7
Water Quality Monitoring Data

After you have collected and recorded your water quality data on *RiverBank,* please e-mail your RiverBank Datasheets to our Watershed Data Coordinator before the end of the month. After receiving the Datasheets from all of the participating schools, she will compile this information and send it back to each school by the middle of next month.

If you want to discuss the results of your tests, or the tests completed by any other member of the program, please use TOPIC 8.

◀ | ◀ | ▶ | ▶| | ● | ⚲ | ⊘ | 👁 | 🐛 | ⚗ | ↕ | □ | ?

Chemical Tests

1,01/31/96, Brever Creek

Test Not Performed	Test Result	Q-Value	Weighing Factor	Total
☐ Dissolved Oxygen (% sat)	12.000	9.888	0.17	1.538
☐ Fecal Coliform (/100ml)	23.000	60.688	0.16	9.789
☐ pH (units)	6.000	55.828	0.11	6.148
☐ B.O.D. (mg/l)	2.000	77.968	0.11	8.576
☐ Δ Temperature (C)	12.000	36.988	0.10	3.698
☐ Total Phosphates (mg/l)	8.000	7.518	0.10	0.751
☐ Nitrates (mg/l)	23.000	33.638	0.10	3.363
☐ Turbidity (in)	1.000	15.518	0.08	1.241
☒ Total Solids (mg/l)	0.000	0.000	0.07	0.000

Overall Water Quality Index 37.643

[Set Test Results As Default] [Equipment Used >>]

RiverBank Chemical Tests Page

Interpreting the Results

Objectives

- Calculate the Water Quality Index, an overall measure of water quality, for your site
- Evaluate the water quality of your site

Materials

- data from your test site
- the **Field Manual for Water Quality Monitoring**
- data from other test sites (if available)
- blackboard or large sheets of paper
- pens, markers, etc.

Time

40-80 minutes to interpret and analyze the data

Background Information

As was the case for Activity 4, the suggestions offered here are very brief. They are designed to help you organize your classroom activities and to provide suggestions for appropriate discussion topics. You will need to draw heavily upon Chapter 3 and Chapter 4 in the **Field Manual for Water Quality Monitoring** in order to analyze your results.

Center for Teaching
The Westminster Schools

| Figure 14. Using hand calculator to help determine the overall water quality index.

Procedure

Physical-chemical Tests

1. Review "Chapter 4: Calculating the Results" in the **Field Manual for Water Quality Monitoring.** This section describes how to compute "Q-values" for each test (a value from 0-100 which reflects the quality of the test result) and an overall "Water Quality Index" for your site. Discuss this procedure with the class and then assign groups of students to perform the calculations.

2. Discuss with students the meaning of the Water Quality Index. Consider the following questions:

   a. Are your results consistent with what students observed in the field?

   b. Do they make sense given where your site is located, relative to industries, agriculture, or human populations?

   c. What tests have particularly low Q-values? Why?

   d. If you have available data from prior years, how does this year's results compare with earlier results?

3. If possible, obtain Water Quality Index values from other test sites in your watershed (see Computer Conference Ideas below). Select a vari-

ety of sites which reflect a diversity of locations and land uses within the watershed.

a. Create a large map of the watershed on the blackboard or on paper (use your watershed map developed in Activity 1 as a guide).

b. Note the approximate locations on the map of the sampling sites selected; for each of these points, list the dominant land uses in that area and the Water Quality Index values.

   1) Are there any noticeable patterns in the variation of Water Quality Index values as you move downstream within the watershed?

   2) Do changes in Water Quality Index Values seem to correspond to land use or any other factors?

   3) Were any of the test results surprising to you? (For example, extremely high "Q-value" for fecal coliform at a specific site). What factors may contribute to this result? (Sewage effluent, sampling error, etc.)

4. Based upon a preliminary analysis of data from your site and other test sites, what do you think are some of the most significant water quality issues facing your community and the entire watershed?

Biological Monitoring

1. Review "Chapter 6: Benthic Macroinvertebrates" in the **Field Manual for Water Quality Monitoring,** especially the latter half of the chapter which describes how to interpret the results of benthic sampling. Compute the index of water quality which corresponds to your sampling method. Discuss the following questions with your class:

a. How does the biological monitoring index you calculated compare with your overall Water Quality Index (from physical-chemical tests) for your site? Are they similar ? Why or why not?

b. What, if anything, can biological monitoring reveal which is not reflected in physical-chemical testing?

2. On the map you constructed for the physical-chemical test results, or on another map, record the results from sampling benthics at several sites within the watershed. Use these questions to stimulate discussion:

a. Do you notice any patterns in water quality throughout the watershed, as indicated by benthic sampling? How does land use influence index values?

b. Did all the schools use the same index? Are there any problems with comparing results from different sites, using different indices?

Sharing Information
Computer Network Ideas

The computer network is an extremely valuable tool to use in comparing data among different parts of the watershed. Have students summarize analyses of their data, and enter it as a response to Topic 8. Next, work with your students to evaluate the test results from several different sites. In what ways are they different from the results your class obtained? How are they similar? What factors contribute to these similarities and differences?

Topic 8

Analyzing the Data

This topic will be used to discuss the results of the water quality monitoring data all of the participants have gathered.

According to the monitoring you did, what are some of the most significant water quality problems facing your section of the watershed? What local land uses or other factors might be contributing to these problems?

How do the results from the benthic samples you took compare with those from the physical-chemical tests; do they suggest similar water quality for a given section of the river? Why or why not?

Also use this topic to clarify any test results you have questions about.

PART III

Problem-Solving

Overview

Rivers around the world face a collection of complex problems. Increased water demand by humans, deforestation, inadequate treatment of animal and human wastes, and toxic contamination all contribute to problems of water quality.

We believe that it is important for students to learn how to confront these complex problems in creative ways. Solving problems and taking action can help students realize that their knowledge, talents, and efforts are worthwhile. Activities that encourage problem-solving and action-taking may be a very satisfying way for students to conclude their water quality monitoring program.

The activities in this section are designed to offer paths to awaken student concern; give students tools to gather more information; build problem solving skills vital to the future; and instill in students a greater sense of confidence in their abilities. They are structured in such a way as to help lead students through the process of problem-solving and action-taking. The activities include:

➤ *Activity 6:* Identifying Specific Problems

➤ *Activity 7:* Visualizing the Future

➤ *Activity 8:* Selecting an Issue to Address

➤ *Activity 9:* Contacting Organizations and Decision Makers

➤ *Activity 10:* Developing an Action Plan

➤ *Activity 11:* Taking Action

➤ *Activity 12:* Follow-up

Figure 15. Rivers in parts of Bangkok, Thailand are lined with homes. Many waterways receive untreated wastes and pose health hazards.

We recommend that you use all of these activities, in the order given, with student groups that plan to take action. However, if your class is not going to undertake a major action project, consider using Activity 7: Visualizing the Future, and Activity 9: Contacting Organizations and Decision Makers. These two activities are useful exercises by themselves, and provide students with an introduction to some problem-solving skills.

Activity

Identifying Specific Problems

Objectives

- Analyze and evaluate water quality information
- Synthesize students' ideas and impressions
- Identify root causes of water pollution
- Build skills working in groups

Materials

- pencil
- paper
- blackboard or newsprint paper

Time

approximately 80 minutes

Background Information

Once students have collected water quality and land use information from a variety of sources, they may be concerned about specific problems they have discovered. This activity gives them a chance to synthesize the information they have gathered and begin to ask themselves, "What are the most serious threats to water quality? What are their root causes?"

Procedure

1. Divide students into small groups for a brainstorming activity. Ask students to use all the information available to them (including their own test results, test results from other schools obtained through the

Figure 16. Brainstorming water quality issues resulting from river investigations.

computer conference, direct observations, the **Field Manual for Water Quality Monitoring,** etc.) to generate a list of problems that impact the river.

2. Once the groups have created their lists of problems, have representatives from each group share their lists with the rest of the class. Generate a master list of major issues, drawn from the students' lists, on the blackboard or on a sheet of paper.

3. Next, review the list with students, and for each one discuss the problem in some detail.

    a. Help your students distinguish between the more obvious, immediate cause of a problem, and the various levels of underlying root causes (which are usually not so obvious). For example, students may have identified a problem like a very high fecal coliform count at one spot along the river. From their field work they can identify that the immediate direct cause of this problem is a point source of organic pollution from a leaky sewer pipe. But what are some of the possible root causes of this problem? Students might conjecture that the local city government, responsible for repairing the pipe, has not done so due to budget constraints. This is one root cause of the pollution problem.

    b. If possible, have students identify even another root cause of the problem, at a deeper level than the first one. For the example given above, the fact that the city cannot afford to fix the sewer pipe may be traced to the budget priorities in the community. Perhaps water quality is less important to decision makers than social service programs, or development, etc.

c. If students have trouble identifying root causes, ask them to fill in the blanks of the following sentence for each problem they identified:

_____ is/are the result of
problem

_____ which is caused by
immediate, direct cause

_____.

root cause

For the example described above, a possible answer would be:

High fecal coliform levels is/are the result of
problem

point source pollution from leaky pipes which is caused by
immediate, direct cause

uninspected sewer lines due to budget constraints
root cause

d. Encourage students to come up with a root cause of a problem even if they do not have enough information to be certain if it is truly an important factor. Later they will have the opportunity to research a problem in greater detail (Activity 9). The purpose of this activity is to get students to think critically, to help them appreciate and understand the complexity of environmental problems, so that when they move onto action taking, they will tackle the sources of a problem, rather than simply treating its symptoms.

Sharing Information
Computer Network Ideas

Have students use the computer conference to share their findings on root and immediate causes of specific problems. They may wish to begin by sharing their list of problems with other schools and asking for feedback on possible causes. They can then follow up by revealing their own hypotheses.

Use the World Wide Web as a research tool for finding information and/or experts to aid in understanding your local water quality data. As a starting point for exploration, visit GREEN's WWW site at <http://www.igc.apc.org/green>.

As you identify experts, or other groups working on similar watershed issues, involve them in your research by having students write e-mail messages asking specific questions. Post the student queries and other responses received in your on-line forum.

Compare and contrast how problems are perceived by different people and different communities. Do professionals view problems the same way as students? Do rural residents view the problems the same way as urban residents? How do different cultures perceive the same problems?

Topic 9

Specific Problems in the Watershed

Based upon the water quality monitoring data you collected and analyzed, or other experiences with the river, what are some of the major water quality problems you are concerned about? For each problem you identify, list what you think are some of the underlying, root causes of the problem.

Activity

Visualizing the Future

Objectives

- Visualize future state of your river or stream
- Promote written and artistic expression
- Apply previous experiences to a new activity

Materials

- ◆ pencil
- ◆ paper

- ◆ colored pencils and paints (optional)

Time

approximately 40 minutes

Background Information

Visualization is a technique used by individuals to improve their performance. For example, athletes rehearse in their minds the sequence of steps required in their sport. Visualization can also be used by people to help solve problems, and to envision solutions.

In this activity, students will develop their personal vision of a watercourse. What are their hopes for the future condition of the river? What changes would they like to see in how humans impact the river system? Encourage students to draw upon their prior experiences with the river or stream—mapping, interviewing people and water quality monitoring—as they visualize the future.

| Figure 17. Visualizing what the river might be like in fifteen years.

Procedure

1. Have students visualize how they would like the river to be in the future, and record their thoughts, feelings and impressions in writing and/or art. Some suggestions that may be helpful to students are:

   a. Clear your mind for writing. A moment of silence can help you to focus on this activity.

   b. Reflect upon your experiences and knowledge of the river or stream—think of both positives and negatives.

   c. Try to be specific in writing down your thoughts. " I want the river to be clean" does not convey much information. Why do you want a clean river? So that people can swim in the river, or safely use it for drinking?

   d. Discuss changes or improvements that you would like to see. Words like "reduce," "eliminate," "improve," and "increase" demonstrate movement or changes.

   e. Consider young people in the next generation, 20-30 years from now. What kind of a river would you like them to experience?

   f. You may want to assume the role of a fish, or other organism. What kind of an aquatic environment would the fish like? What are some changes that would have to occur?

2. With students' permission, personal visions could be shared with the entire group. Student writings and art will convey goals and aspira-

tions for the river that are shared by many students. Some ideas for achieving these goals will emerge within the writings and can serve as the groundwork for gathering further information on water quality problems, and designing an action plan.

Sharing Information
Computer Network Ideas

Your students could share their personal visions with other students through the computer conference. How do students' visions vary throughout the watershed? What goals do the students have in common?

Topic 10

Future Visions for the Watershed

Would you like to see any changes in the water quality of the river in the future? Why or why not?

What are your personal visions for the future state of the river in 10, 20, 30, 50, or 100 years?

What types of activities (for example recreation, industry, agriculture, etc.) would you like to see happening along the river that are not occurring now?

Activity

Selecting an Issue to Address

Objectives

- Develop problem-solving skills: prioritizing problems and generating criteria for selecting one issue to address
- Build group process skills: making choices by discussion and consensus
- Enhance analytical skills: clearly defining and stating the problem chosen

Materials

- List of problems and root causes generated in the previous activity
- blackboard or sheets of paper

Time

approximately 80 minutes

Background Information

In the previous activity, students generated a list of problems that affect the river and identified one or more root causes for each. If students wish to take action to solve any of these problems, they will need to spend some time selecting criteria to narrow their choices and then choose one issue to address.

Figure 18. Small groups review criteria for selecting a class issue.

The purpose of this activity is to help students focus on the criteria that make an issue appropriate for them to tackle. After selecting an issue, they are asked to clearly define and state the problem they chose.

Procedure

1. Have students generate criteria for selecting a problem to act upon. Some useful criteria are:

   a. Is the problem relevant and of high interest to everyone in the class?

   b. Is there adequate information about the problem?

   c. Are other people or organizations already working on the problem? (this can be very useful, since other organizations may have information and access to resources students can tap).

   d. Is the problem too large or too complex for student action? If so, can it be redefined, or simplified in such a way that students can take meaningful action(s) to address the problem?

   e. What kinds of resources will students need to tackle this problem? Are these resources available?

   f. What is the group's time frame for working on this project?

   g. What kind of action will most likely be appropriate for solving this problem? Is this level of action feasible for students?

2. Evaluate the list of problems in light of these criteria.

3. Next, have students agree on a problem to address.

4. Students should then work together to develop a precise statement of the issue they have selected. Encourage students to make as many additional refinements to the problem definition as necessary at this point.

5. Students should define what they see as a successful outcome of their action(s).

6. Finally, have the entire class evaluate and critique this problem statement.

Sharing Information — Computer Network Ideas

Some schools may not be involved in long-term action projects and thus will not be selecting an issue to address. However, it is a valuable exercise to categorize and prioritize important water quality problems in your area. Use the conference to discuss the nature of these problems in greater detail.

If your class is undertaking an action project, communicate the problem statement to other schools through Topic 11, and ask for responses: "Is the problem statement clear? What suggestions do other schools have to offer for help in solving the problem?" Students may wish to use the computer conference to invite other schools to join them in addressing the problem. It can be a useful tool for sharing research findings and ideas.

Topic 11

Selecting an Issue for Further Investigation

In TOPIC 9 a whole list of specific water quality problems facing rivers in the watershed was generated. This topic is for discussing some of these problems in greater detail.

Which problems in the watershed are most important and require immediate attention? Share why you think a given problem deserves further investigation. What criteria did you use in selecting the problem?

If your school has decided to address an issue through an action project, identify the problem for others on the conference.

Activity

Contacting Organizations and Decision-Makers

Objectives

- Identify community resources
- Gather information related to the problem selected
- Develop phone and personal interviewing techniques
- Learn how to write effective letters

Materials

- Newspapers
- telephone directories
- government directories

- reference books
- periodicals, etc.

Time

40-80 minutes (This process could potentially take longer, depending upon how much research the students need do. Ideally, much of their work can be assigned as homework over the course of several days).

Background Information

This activity is designed to help students develop basic research skills which are essential to effective problem-solving. It is important for students to learn to gather information from diverse sources and to critically evaluate this information, if they are to resolve environmental problems.

This activity can be used to help your students research the problem they selected in Activity 8. The research they conduct will likely provide them with a better understanding of the problem, and prepare them for later

---

Figure 19. Use of school library to collect relevant information on selected issue.

developing an action plan (Activity 10). In classes that are not undertaking major actions, this activity could be used simply as an exercise to help students improve research skills.

Procedure

1. Students will likely have raised many difficult questions throughout the course of the previous activities. Now they have the chance to search out some answers. Have students, in small groups or by themselves, generate a list of questions and issues that concern them. If your class is working on an action project, it may be appropriate to discuss these with the entire group: prioritize the information your class needs in order to better understand and work towards a resolution of their chosen problem.

2. Next, discuss what agencies or individuals would be appropriate to contact in order to find answers to their questions.

    a. Good contacts include: natural resource or environmental agencies, environmental organizations, local municipal governments, industries, public works departments, etc.

    b. If students are having difficulty figuring out who to contact, suggest they use resources such as: phone directories; governmental directories, periodicals; newspapers; other reference books; and the local library.

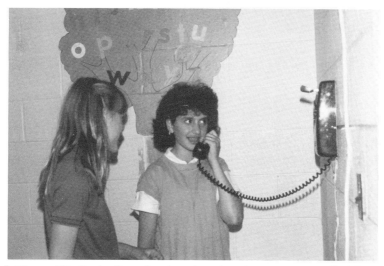

Figure 20. Contacting planning department to request staff visit to explain high fecal coliform counts in local river.

3. Once students have identified contact persons or organizations, the next step is to phone, write or visit (whatever is most appropriate for the situation). It is helpful to have students role play what they will say, and read their letters aloud to get feedback from other students.

4. Remind students to ask contacts for other information "leads." Often, people working in regulatory agencies or other governmental organizations have developed a network of contacts that students might also utilize.

5. Have students report the results of their inquiries to the whole class. Be certain to discuss and analyze the information that each student (or group of students) presents.

6. Some additional suggestions:

   a. Because of their interdisciplinary nature, complex issues may require several rounds of information gathering. Encourage patience and persistence on the part of your students!

   b. Keep a record of phone numbers and addresses, when people were contacted, and the subject of the conversation or letter for later referral.

   c. Consider asking one or more contact persons to make a presentation to the class. This is an excellent way for students to learn about an issue.

| Figure 21. Writing a letter using school's "Guide to Letter Preparation."

Sharing Information
Computer Network Ideas

Valuable contacts may be reached via the computer. The computer is also an effective means to share contact names and ideas for possible resources with other participating schools.

Topic 12

Resources for Gathering Information

If you were to address one of the problems facing your local river (or the watershed) you would need to first gather some more information about that specific problem. What are some of the resources you might contact to learn more about water quality issues in your area?

Figure 22. Battery operated computers are useful in gathering data while in the field.

Activity

Developing an Action Plan

Objectives

- Identify a variety of potential actions to resolve the identified problem
- Select an appropriate and viable action (or actions) to implement
- Outline specific steps in the implementation process
- Build group decision-making skills
- Develop research skills

Materials

- Blackboard
- paper
- pencils

Time

 approximately 120 minutes

Background Information

Once students have selected a problem and conducted some prelimi-nary research, the next step is to develop an action plan to solve it. It is very important that the class carefully determine realistic goals and objectives for the action plan. How will the students know when they have been success-ful? In other words, how should they define success?

Perhaps students will have very ambitious goals for their class project. Students and teachers will need to determine what is feasible for the class to

Figure 23. Practicing presentation to be given to water resources agency, using TV monitor to critique talk.

undertake. Raising awareness in classmates about a pollution issue in itself is a viable project goal. However, solving any environmental problem is challenging and time-consuming, requiring commitment and patience. But if the class has thoughtfully identified a problem and has set realistic goals for the action plan, the problem-solving experience should be very rewarding and exciting.

Procedure

1. Have students brainstorm possible actions to address their chosen problem. They may benefit from learning more about the various levels of action-taking available to them. You can provide students with a matrix of possible actions including:

    a. Persuasion—used to try and convince others that a certain course of action is correct, or that certain behaviors need to change. Persuasion can take the form of a logical reporting of facts, experiential awareness-building, or an emotional appeal. Examples include letters to the editor, presentations to classmates, parents, school boards, or city council members, posters, etc. Most strategies include some form of persuasion.

    b. Consumerism—This involves buying or not buying a product in order to influence the producers' behavior. It is usually effective only when a group of people agree to act together. Perhaps a class could try and convince parents and other students to stop buying hazardous household products by providing examples of non-hazardous alternatives.

Figure 24. Checking store products for environmentally safe alternatives.

    c. Political Action—includes any strategy that pressures political groups or government to take a certain action. Distributing petitions, letter-writing to political figures, supporting an environmental referendum, and speaking before the city council or school board are all examples of political action.

    d. Eco-management—any physical action that improves the environment is eco-management. Campaigns to pick up trash along the riverbanks, replant eroded banks, or dislodge log-jams are typical eco-management strategies.

2. Another way to help your class prepare an effective action plan is to have them learn from the experiences of others.

3. After students have generated possible strategies, they should develop action-taking criteria, just as they did to select an appropriate problem. Some criteria to consider include:

    a. How many steps does this strategy involve?

    b. Does this strategy involve the whole class?

    c. How will the community react to this action strategy?

    d. What level of intervention is being considered? Is the action aimed at personal changes, school level changes, or larger-scale changes in the community?

𝔇𝔢𝔱𝔯𝔬𝔦𝔱 𝔉𝔯𝔢𝔢 𝔓𝔯𝔢𝔰𝔰

Section A, Page 3　　　SECOND FRONT PAGE　　　Sunday, May 17, 1987 •

Human wastes found in Rouge

Effluent in river despite dry period

By JOEL THURTELL
Free Press Staff Writer

When students from 16 high schools in Wayne and Oakland counties tested Rouge River water earlier this month they found enough old tires, junked cars, shopping carts and empty beer bottles to stock a town dump.

They also found the unexpected — human waste flowing into the Rouge from a sewer in Farmington Hills even though it was dry weather.

"We found that our river is as bad as we thought it would be. We found no living organisms," wrote River Rouge High School student Maliika Noland. "There were oil slicks floating on top of the water, and garbage. The water was dark green and smelled very bad."

Effluent entering the river during rainy periods may be disgusting, but that's how the system was designed in the 1940s and 1950s — to let storm drains conduct sewage to the river at times of peak water flow.

But the dry weather sewage measurements by North Farmington High School students on May 7 shocked James Murray, the Washtenaw County drain commissioner who also is chairman of the State Water Resources Commission and president of Friends of the Rouge, a private group dedicated to improving water quality in the Rouge.

"It tells you the CSO (combined sewer overflow) has got crap going out of it, and that's illegal during dry water flow," Murray said.

HE DISCUSSED implications of the water test results Saturday at Detroit's Redford High School with about 50 students from the 16 Rouge basin high schools participating in the Interactive Rouge River Water Quality Project sponsored by Friends of the Rouge.

But even before Saturday's meeting, students from North Farmington High wrote in the project's computer bulletin board that "we are having the city engineer of the city of Farmington Hills come to our class May 28 for us to learn of of the present system here and for us to share our data with him. Our CSO was still draining days after the last rain."

Erin English, a 16-year-old sophomore biology student from Redford Union High School, described her efforts at drawing water samples from the Rouge's upper branch: "It was really gross — we saw a couple of tires in the water. We didn't see any fish."

Data from the 16 student groups showed consistently increasing degradation along the river, said William Stapp, a University of Michigan natural resources professor who directed the project.

The Rouge runs from upland streams merging in Oakland County to its mouth near Zug Island in River Rouge. More than 1.5 million people live in the Rouge River basin.

Sewage was well below levels considered dangerous for swimming in Novi, Birmingham and Plymouth, but fecal coliform levels increase steadily as the river flows downstream. Near the river's mouth, a student group measured fecal coliform 127 times higher than the maximum level allowed for swimming and 25 times higher than the level allowed for boating. The levels were 25,400 times higher than the maximum level allowed for

Figure 25. Class members spoke to newspapers staff writer about results of their river study, resulting in a major article in local newspaper.

4. Next, students should select one or more action strategies based upon a consideration of these criteria. Be extremely conscious of the issue of success. If students select a strategy which they cannot possibly follow-through on due to time or logistical constraints, they will feel very discouraged. This may be the first experience with problem-solving for many students; help reduce their likelihood of failure, so that they become excited about future problem-solving opportunities.

5. After students have selected an appropriate action strategy, they should again clearly state the problem and the strategy they have adopted to solve it.

6. Finally, have the class develop a time-line and list of step-by-step procedures to aid in implementing their action plan. Consider also what kinds of additional information might be helpful to the students.

Figure 26. Conondale State School in Australia, collaborated with local governmental departments in a river rehabilitation project

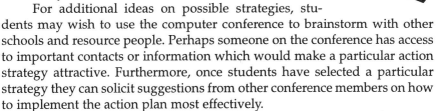

Sharing Information
Computer Network Ideas

Previously your class identified water quality problems, then discussed visions for the future of the river. Now they have the opportunity to come up with possible actions which can help translate their visions into reality.

For additional ideas on possible strategies, students may wish to use the computer conference to brainstorm with other schools and resource people. Perhaps someone on the conference has access to important contacts or information which would make a particular action strategy attractive. Furthermore, once students have selected a particular strategy they can solicit suggestions from other conference members on how to implement the action plan most effectively.

Topic 13

Actions to Improve Water Quality

What are some of the types of actions you can take to address the water quality problems in your community, or in the entire watershed? What personal lifestyle changes can you make which will help improve water quality in the river? Do you know of any actions that other group have taken to deal with similar problems? If so, describe them.

Activity

Taking Action

Objectives

● Implement the students' action plan

Materials

◆ All the materials used previously may be needed, depending on the problem and actions chosen

Time

Varies considerably depending on the nature of the students' project

---

Background Information

The action phase of the problem-solving process is typically a simultaneously exciting and frustrating experience. But with patience and commitment, it will hopefully be a rewarding one as well for both you and your students.

The specific nature of your students' project will determine how to best go about implementing their action plan. However, we provide some general guidelines below which you may find useful.

Procedure

1. Utilize the students' action plan to guide their activities. Refer to the time-line and list of step-by-step procedures developed in Activity 9.

Figure 27. Drawing a poster for local mall to encourage citizens to recycle car oil rather than release the oil into a storm drain directed toward the river.

2. Be sensitive to the frustrations and difficulties students may experience. Support them and encourage them constantly.

3. Encourage students to be considerate of conflicting viewpoints. If the project goal is at all controversial, students can expect some people (perhaps even members of the class) to resist their efforts. Students should try to think broadly and empathize with a number of perspectives as they proceed. Have them consider the following questions:

   a. Who will welcome our project and why?

   b. Who will oppose the project and why?

   c. Who might not listen to our statements? What is our best approach with these people?

   d. How can we better understand other people's views?

4. What special planning or preparation does the students' project require?

   a. Will the project involve making a presentation at a local government meeting or to a board of directors? This could offer students an excellent opportunity to experience participatory democracy and develop public speaking skills. Students can do role-plays or mock meetings to get ready for their presentations.

Figure 28. Water quality study culminating in an article printed in the school newspaper.

b. Will the project require significant research off school property like visits to sewage treatment plants, etc.? You will need to consider issues of safety, parental permission, and liability. It might be wise to visit the site before taking the students there to look for sources of potential problems.

c. Will the project involve the use of the media? Often local newspapers can be helpful to a project by increasing public awareness of an issue. However, be certain to obtain parental permission before using pictures or interviews of students in publicity efforts.

Sharing Information
Computer Network Ideas

Students will have much to discuss on the computer conference as they experience the excitement and frustration of implementing their action plan. Encourage students to share successes and provide inspiration to other groups, and to ask for advice and feedback if help is needed.

Topic 14

Taking Action: Opportunities and Constraints

This topic is for discussing actions we can take to address the water quality problems identified in previous topics. If your class is undertaking an action project, share some of your experiences. What are you doing? What problems have you run into? Is there any opposition to your action plan? Any support? What impact have your actions had?

Activity

Follow-Up

Objectives

- Evaluate the effectiveness of the students' action pro-ject (if appropriate)
- Evaluate the water quality monitoring program
- Describe the problem solving process
- Consider the applicability of skills gained from involvement in a water quality monitoring program to future attempts at problem solving

Materials

- ◆ Paper
- ◆ blackboard or poster board

- ◆ pens

Time

 approximately 40-80 minutes

Background Information

Evaluation of the students' action project and the entire water quality monitoring program (the whole series of activities they have been involved) is a very important part of the learning process. Both you and the students will benefit from a critical assessment of the impact(s) of their actions, and a sharing of thoughts and feelings about the program.

This wrap-up should serve as an affirmation of the hard but mean-ingful work students have done. It will also likely highlight some of the

Figure 29. An open evaluation of the entire water quality monitoring program with teacher and students.

problems they encountered and lead to suggestions which will facilitate future attempts at problem solving.

Procedure

Evaluation of the Action Project

1. Have your class evaluate the effectiveness of their action project using the "plus-minus-change" method:

    a. On the blackboard or a large piece of paper create three columns and label them "plus," "minus," and "change."

    b. Consider the question "How well did our action address the problem we identified?" Ask students to list what they liked about the action project under the "plus" column and what they did not like under "minus." The "change" column is for listing any changes they would like to make; how the action could have been improved.

    c. You can join in this activity by offering your feedback as well.

2. Have students reflect on the problem solving process they used.

    a. Have each student write down a brief:

        1) Restatement of the problem they decided to work on

        2) Outline of the procedure they followed to address the problem

3) Summary of their action plan

4) Description of the result of their actions.

b. Lead a discussion in which students share their depiction's of the problem solving process. Use the following questions as a guide:

1) Do students' perceptions of the problem solving process differ? If so, why? (Was there adequate communication in the class? Was everyone fully involved throughout the entire program?)

2) What part of the problem solving process was most difficult or frustrating ? Why? What can you do in the future to make it easier?

3) How did you feel when you completed the action project? Were you successful? Why or why not?

Evaluation of the Water Quality Monitoring Program

1. Follow the same procedure for a "plus-minus-change" evaluation outlined above, but focus this time on the entire program—the whole series of activities students were involved in, including their action project.

2. Assign each student to write an essay in which they share their personal thoughts and feelings about their involvement in the program. Ask them to consider some specific questions, such as:

a. What did you like most about working with this program? Why?

b. What did you like least? Why?

c. What did you learn from these activities?

d. Can you and other students your age do anything to help solve water quality problems? Why or why not?

Sharing Information ————————
Computer Network Ideas

Have your class share the results of their evaluations with other student groups. Ask members of the conference to summarize what they learned from their action project. How can they apply this knowledge to future attempts at problem solving?

Here, it may be valuable to coordinate schedules with other on-line partners so that students can "celebrate" their successes with a "party" in your on-line forum over a one or two day period.

Figure 30. Native Americans in communication with neighboring bands in the Great Lakes Basin.

Topic 15

Evaluation

How do you feel about being involved in this water quality monitoring project? What parts of it have you enjoyed the most? What has been most difficult or frustrating for you? What have you learned from this experience?

References

Bardwell, Lisa; Monroe, Martha; and Tudor, Margaret. (1994). *Environmental Problem Solving: Theory, Practice and Possibilities in Environmental Education*, North American Association for Environmental Education, Troy, OH.

Beringer, Almut; Stapp, William; Wals, Arjen. (1990). Education in Action: A Community Problem Solving Study for Schools. *Journal of Environmental Education*. 21(4): 13-20.

Carr, W. and S. Kemmis. (1896). *Becoming Critical: Education, Knowledge and Action Research*. London, Falmer Press.

Connell, S. (1985). *Teacher's Work*. Sydney Australia: Allen and Unwin. pp. 128-147.

Corey, S.M. (1953). *Action Research to Improve School Practices*. New York, Teachers' College Press.

Dewey, J. (1963) *Experience & Education*. Collier Books, Macmillan Publishing Company, NY.

Dewey, J. (1965). Relating Theory to Practice in Education. In: Borrowman, M.L. (Ed.) *Teacher Education in America: A Documentary History*. New York, Teachers' College Press.

Di Chiro, G. and Stapp, W.B. (1986). Education in Action: An Action Research Approach to Environmental Problem Solving. In Perkins, J.H., Alexis, D., and Bauer, K. (Eds.), *Monographs in Environmental Education and Environmental Studies*, Vol. III. Troy, Ohio: The North American Association for Environmental Education.

Ellis, Thomas; Wals, Arjen; and Cromwell, Mare. (1991). *Global Education through Local Involvement: The Global Rivers Environmental Education Network*. Journal of Environmental Education, Winter Issue, Troy, OH.

Gitilin, A. and K. Teitelbaum. (1983). Linking Theory and Practice. *Journal of Education for Teaching*. 9(3): 225-234.

Greenall Gough, A. and Robottom, I. (1990). *Environmental Education and the Socially Critical School*. Deakin University Mimeo, Geelong, Victoria, Deakin University, Australia.

Greig, S., Pike, G. and Selby, D. (1987). *Earthrights: Education as if the Planet Really Mattered*. World Wildlife Fund, Kogan Page, London.

Hammond, W. (1986). *The Monday Group: From Awareness to Action*. In: Project Wild Teacher Guide, pg. 276-283.

Hustler, D. et al. (1986). *Action Research in Classrooms and Schools.* Allen & Unwin, London.

Kemmis, S. (1985). *Action Research,* In: Husen, T. and T. Posthlethwaite (eds.). International Encyclopedia of Education: Research and Studies, Volume 1, A-B, Oxford, Pergamon.

Kemmis, S.; Cole, P.; and Suggett, D. (1983). *Orientations to Curriculum and Transition: Towards the Socially Critical School.* Melbourne, Victorian Institute of Secondary Education.

King, M. L. Jr. (1964). *Strength to Love.* Pocket Books, Inc. NY.

Mitchell, Mark and William Stapp. (1996). *Field Manual for Water Quality Monitoring* (10th Edition). Thomson-Shore, Dexter MI.

Mitchell, Mark and William Stapp. (1995). *Interactive Rouge River Water Quality Monitoring.* University of Michigan Symposium, Ann Arbor, MI.

Monroe, M. C. *Converting "It's No Use into "Hey, There's a Lot I Can Do:" A Matrix for Environmental Action Taking.* In Simmons, D. A.; Knapp, C. and Young, C. (Eds.) Setting the EE Agenda for the 90's, 1990 Conference Proceedings. Troy, OH; NAAEE, 1990.

Naisbitt, J. (1982). *Megatrends.* New York, Warner Books.

Riel, Margaret M. and James A. Levin. (1990). "Building Education Communities: Success and Failure in Computer Networking." Instructional Science (19):145-169.

Robottom, Ian. (1985). School-Based Environmental Education: An Action Research Report. *Journal of Environmental Education and Information.* United Kingdom.

Robottom, I. (1987). Towards Inquiry-Based Professional Development in Environmental Education. In: Robottom, I. (Ed.). *Environmental Education: Practice and Possibility.* Deakin University Press, Victoria, Australia.

Rogers, C. (1983). *Freedom to Learn for the 80's.* Columbus, OH., Merrill.

Rumelhardt, D.E. and D.A. Norman. (1981). Analogical Processes in Learning. In: J.R. Anderson (Ed.). *Cognitive Skills and their Acquisition.* Lawrence Erlbaum and Associates.

Stapp. W. B. and E. J. Wals. (1994). *An Action Research Approach to Environmental Problem Solving*. In: Bardwell, L.V., Monroe, M.C., and M.T. Tudor (Eds.). Environmental Problem Solving: Theory, Practice and Possibilities in Environmental Education. Troy, OH. North American Association for Environmental Education.

Stapp, William and Wals, Arjen (1995). *The Global Rivers Environmental Education Network*. In International Environmental Education Case Studies. Edited by Susan Jacobs, University of Forida State Press.

Stapp, William and Mark Mitchell (1995). *Field Manual for Global Low-cost Water Quality Monitoring*. Thomson-Shore Printers, Dexter, MI.

Toffler, A. (1974). *Learning for Tomorrow: The Role of the Future in Education*. New York, Vintage.

UNESCO (1977). *Intergovernmental Conference on Environmental Education*. Tbilisi, Russia. UNESCO Press, Paris, France.

Wals, A. E. J., Beringer, A. R., and W. B. Stapp, *Education in Action: A Community Problem Solving Program in Schools*. Journal of Environmental Education, 21, (4), 13-19, Summer 1990.

Wals, A. E. J.; Monroe, Martha; and Stapp, William. (1990). *Computers: Bridging Troubled Waters*. In "Computer-Aided Environmental Education," Edited by W. J. Rohwedder, North American Association for Environmental Education, Volume VII, Troy OH.

Wals, A. E. J. (1994). *Action Taking and Environmental Problem Solving*. In: Jensen, B and K. Schnack, "Action and Action Competence as Key Concepts in Critical Pedagogy." Copenhagen: Royal School of Educational Studies.

Wals, A. E. J. (1994). *Pollution Stinks! Young Adolescents' Perception of Environmental Issues: Implication for Environment Education in Urban Settings*, De Lier: Academic Book Center, 1994.

Winter, R. (1989). *Learning from Experiences: Principles and Practices in Action Research*. New York: Falmer Press.

GREEN
Global Rivers Environmental Education Network
Global citizens sharing their concerns for water quality

GREEN is an innovative, action-oriented approach to education, based on an interdisciplinary watershed education model. GREEN's mission is to improve education through a global network that promotes watershed sustainability. It is a resource to schools and communities that wish to study their watershed and work to improve their quality of life.

GREEN works closely with educational and environmental organizations, community groups, businesses, and government across the United States and Canada, and in over 130 countries around the globe to support local efforts in watershed education and sustainability.

Students at North Farmington High School near Detroit detected elevated levels of bacterial contamination down river from a pipe exiting a City sewage pumping station. They presented their findings to the City Engineer, who acted quickly to repair the malfunctioning pump.

GREEN Watershed Education Model

The model involves the synthesis of content and process. Activities revolve around two key areas: watershed and water quality monitoring, and understanding changes and trends within the whole watershed.

GREEN participants collect and analyze real-life environmental data; study current and historical patterns of land and water usage within their watershed; share their data, concerns and strategies for action with others in the watershed and beyond; and develop concrete action plans to improve local water quality.

Key to the GREEN process is an emphasis on creating a learning community of teachers, students, parents, community groups, government, nongovernmental organizations, and businesses—whose members share a vision for watershed sustainability and possess the skills, knowledge, and motivation necessary to create change.

How GREEN Can Help You

GREEN publishes a quarterly, **international newsletter** and a **catalog of educational resources,** hosts a **World Wide Web** home page, sponsors watershed-wide and international **computer conferences** on EcoNet, and connects classrooms internationally in **cross cultural partnerships,** develops and disseminates **watershed education materials,** and provides **training and support** to local watershed education efforts.

GREEN is pioneering a **partnership approach** to educational development and environmental sustainability. Our partners include National Science Foundation, U.S. Department of Education, U.S. EPA, U.S. Fish and Wildlife Service, White House Office of Science and Technology Policy, U.N. Environment Programme, General Motors Corp., Key Bank, Bullitt Foundation, Institute for Global Communications, I*EARN, River Watch Network, TERC, Trout Unlimited, National Project WET, University of Michigan, Western Washington University, American Rivers, Inc, Atlantic Center for the Environment, and the Center for Watershed Protection. Joint research and development initiatives with our partners allow GREEN participants to benefit from the broad array of expertise represented within our network.

One GREEN student described to her father the adverse impacts of allowing his livestock direct access to the stream. He agreed to buy fencing material if she would help him build a fence. They proceeded to build the fence adjacent to the stream and followed up by planting trees and shrubs to establish a riparian corridor.

GREEN Workshops and Institutes

GREEN can help you start or enhance your watershed education program. We'll create and deliver a **Custom Workshop** with support materials to fit the goals of your program and participants. Topics include:

➤ Starting a Watershed Education Program
➤ Interdisciplinary Approaches to Watershed Education
➤ Water Quality Monitoring & Data Interpretation

- Land Use Analysis With Maps & Satellite Imagery
- Telecommunications in Watershed Education
- Student Problem Solving & Action Taking

All workshops provide hands-on experience in the GREEN approach for watershed education; a variety of support materials; a basic understanding of the complex relationships between land, water, and people; and activities that demonstrate the importance of protecting the environment and how individuals and communities can effect environmental change.

GREEN also hosts a series of regularly scheduled, introductory **Watershed Education Institutes** at locations across the U.S. and Canada. Please contact GREEN for details.

A local business man working with Project del Rio, an international GREEN program that links schools along the U.S.-Mexico border, is convinced that the GREEN model is "exactly the kind of program that enables a community to participate in the preservation and restoration of its environment."

On the Cutting Edge

GREEN is engaged in numerous initiatives to develop and refine curricular materials and to pilot **innovative approaches to education** such as school-community linkages, inquiry-based learning, action research, use of telecommunications and technology, and cross cultural learning. With our partners we are developing software for modeling environmental data, digital technology for field investigations, Internet-accessible environmental database technology, and low-cost methods for environmental monitoring.

A fundamental part of our research and development strategy is the suite of GREEN publications. GREEN publishes manuals, curriculum guides, and videos to support global watershed education. Our titles cover topics such as: water quality monitoring, action taking, and cross-cultural partnerships. Contact GREEN if you would like to receive our catalog of educational materials and water monitoring equipment.

GREEN Publications

- **Field Manual for Water Quality Monitoring** details nine chemical/physical water quality tests and methods for biological monitoring. It also includes chapters on heavy metals testing, land use practices, action taking, and computer networking. The Field Manual is the foundation for GREEN's Educational Model.

The following books provide more in-depth information on components of their model.

- *Field Manual for Global Low Cost Water Quality Monitoring* provides a global perspective for watershed education. It includes activities to help readers understand key concepts and build skills. It provides handouts and instructions for making inexpensive equipment.

- *Investigating Streams and Rivers* is an activity guide that promotes an interdisciplinary approach to watershed education. It focuses on action taking and enhancing student involvement through computer networks.

- *Sourcebook for Watershed Education* provides detailed guidelines for the development of watershed-wide education programs, focusing on program goals, funding, and school-community partnerships. It contains a rich set of interdisciplinary classroom activities and outlines GREEN's educational philosophy.

- *Cross Cultural Watershed Partners: Activities Manual* contains activities for use in an intercultural watershed education program, and suggestions on how to structure a cross cultural exchange around watershed themes.

- *Air Pollution: Ozone Study and Action* moves students from awareness of air pollution and ozone to a point where they will be knowledgeable and empowered to make action to address problems in their own lives and communities.

- *Environmental Education for Empowerment* enables students, teachers, administrators, and others to effectively participate in the planning, implementation and evaluation of educational activities aimed at resolving an environmental issue that they themselves have identified.

- *International Case Studies on Water Quality Education* provides a rich picture of the kaleidoscope of programs world-wide. These case studies sensitize the reader to potential implementation barriers and offer a vast number of new ideas and resources for school and community based programs. (available late 1996)

- *Heavy Metals Manual* provides background information about heavy metals—ecological effects, sources or metals, policies, and laws. It also provides instructions for bioassay monitoring, instrument techniques and safety procedures. (available late 1996)

About GREEN

The impetus for GREEN began the spring of 1984 with a group of concerned students at a high school located along the polluted Huron River in Ann Arbor, Michigan. Their teacher contacted Dr. William Stapp and other educators at the University of Michigan, and together they developed a comprehensive educational program called GREEN.

The idea quickly caught on; experiences gained in three years of work with schools along the Huron set the stage for an expanded program on the Rouge River in 1987—part of an effort to improve education and the environment in the broader Detroit metropolitan area.

The educational model moved to other watersheds around the Great Lakes in the U.S. and Canada. As the program expanded nationally and then internationally, other components were added: community partnerships, computer telecommunications, cross cultural opportunities, and integration of GREEN's initiatives across the curriculum to form a comprehensive program for watershed sustainability.

Join the GREEN Network

We invite you to become a member of the Global Rivers Environmental Education Network, a community of global citizens dedicated to watershed stewardship and the enhancement of education.

➤ **Student Membership** ($5 per year) makes it possible for GREEN to offer you access to the GREEN World Wide Web home page and a GREEN KIDS membership card.

➤ **Supporting Individual Membership** ($25 per year) makes it possible for GREEN to offer you the quarterly GREEN Newsletter and access to a special rate GREEN/EcoNet Account.

➤ **Contributing Individual Membership** ($50 per year) makes it possible for GREEN to offer you the quarterly GREEN Newsletter, access to a special rate GREEN/EcoNet account, a 10% discount on items in the GREEN Catalog, and a 10% discount on Institutes and Workshops.

➤ **Sustaining Individual Membership** ($100 per year) makes it possible for GREEN to offer you the quarterly GREEN Newsletter, access to a special rate GREEN/EcoNet account, a 15% discount on items in the GREEN catalog, and a 15% discount on Institutes and Workshops.

➤ **Group Membership** ($500 per year and higher, depending on group size) makes it possible for GREEN to offer all group members the quarterly GREEN Newsletter, access to special rate GREEN/EcoNet accounts, a 15% discount on items in the GREEN Catalog, and a 15% discount on Institutes and Workshops. Minimum group size 25; please contact GREEN for details.

You can contact GREEN at:

GREEN
721 E. Huron St., Ann Arbor, MI 48104
USA

Tel: (313) 761-8142
Fax: (313) 761-4951

Internet: green@green.org
WWW: http://www.igc.apc.org/green

I'd Like to Join GREEN

☐ Student Membership $5/yr
☐ Supporting Individual $25/yr
☐ Contributing Individual $50/yr
☐ Sustaining Individual $100/yr

William B. Stapp Endowment Fund

We have initiated a capital campaign honoring **Professor William B. Stapp,** founder and Honorary Director of GREEN. Dr. Stapp is recognized as one of the influential figures in modern environmental education. He served as Director of UNESCO's Environmental Education Program, and as president of the North American Association for Environmental Education. Dr. Stapp is a Nobel Prize nominee and Professor Emeritus at the University of Michigan School of Natural Resources and Environment.

I would like to make a contribution to the **William B. Stapp Endowment Fund.** I have enclosed payment in the amount of $ _____ .

Total Enclosed $ _____

☐ Check Enclosed
☐ Purchase Order # _____
☐ Tax Exemption # (if applicable) _____
☐ Credit Card # _____
     MC   /   Visa (circle one)
     Expiration Date: _____

Signature: _____

Print Name: _____

Address: _____

Tel: _____

Fax: _____

E-mail: _____

Contributions for Membership and to the William B. Stapp Endowment Fund
are tax deductible to the extent allowable by law.